Back

SIMPLIFY LIVING

AMIT BUTANI

Powered by

24by7publishing.com

This book **Back 2 Basics** by Amit Butani is
self-published by the author.
All the printing & distribution process of the book
is powered by

24by7 Publishing
13 New Road, Kolkata - 51, India
https://www.24by7publishing.com
mail@24by7publishing.com
+91 9831 470 133
+91 9433 444 334

MRP: $15

First Published in December, 2020

Version 1.00

ISBN: 978-93-90537-06-8

Powered by

24by7publishing.com

GET YOUR FIRST LIFE TRANSFORMATION SESSION FREE FOR THE FIRST 25 BUYERS!

AMIT BUTANI

Certified
EFT /TFT Practitioner
Life Coach
Eden Energy Medicine Practitioner
Aromatherapist
Akashic Diploma Course

amitbutani@gmail.com
abutani77

TRANSFORMATION
COACH

EMPOWER YOURSELF

DM on my Instagram handle for more details

DEDICATION

FOR EVERYONE WILLING TO EXPERIENCE LIFE TO ITS FULLEST, EXPERIENCING IT IN ALL IT'S GRANDEUR, TAKING CHARGE OF SELF AND CREATING A LIFE OF HAPPINESS AND FULFILMENT.

Table of Contents

Foreword

Hello to the one reading this page!

If you have picked up this book, chances are you have had the pleasure of one of two experiences.

A) You have had the honour of being a ring side witness or cheerleader to the tremendous growth of Amit Butani like myself.

OR

B) The universe believes you are ready for a growth trajectory of your own.

In either case, you have made a choice to read, learn and hopefully be inspired. And that's exactly what this book does. It makes you seek the happiness, peace and health that you see in a man transformed (before your eyes in my case) and hopefully accelerates your own quest in this journey we call life.

The universe is our kindest co-conspirator. Constantly working for our greater good and making sure it's elastic walks spring us back to our meant path. This path leads that very seed, that droplet of spirit to find its way back to the infinite ocean.

Modern western medicine forces us to think of ourselves as a machine made up of several co-functioning organ systems. The human body is so beautiful. It heals – often even in the absence of 'treatment'. It just needs a gentle nudge and the impetuous to want to heal. The Human being is even more fascinating. A feeling, thinking, being, tangible body seeded by intangible emotions, thoughts, intellect and limitless spirit. Wellness therefore depends on healing at physical, emotional, mental and spiritual levels. This gentle and precise guide by Amit Butani that you are holding in your hand is shared wisdom from his experiences to help you lead a more fulfilled, whole and centred life.

This may sound too esoteric, may even initiate that occasional eye roll or giggle from the disbeliever. The truth is you have chosen this life. To be born to certain parents in a certain city to go through certain life experiences that have shaped your thoughts and beliefs. Did you choose disease? Anxiety? Suffering? Poverty? Sadness? Disability? To be born or die during a pandemic? You absolutely did! But you also make a choice every moment of this life to learn, to seek, to overcome and to find yourself.

This beautiful encounter of Amit's life and journey so far is an exploration, a confession and a guidebook all packed in one. He takes us through his "deep night of the soul" which leads him to rediscovering the innate wisdom of his own body and mind.

As humbled as I am to be writing this forward, I feel responsible to motivate you, dear reader, to take the reins of your life in your hands. Use the gentle guidelines of this book to better your mind, body and spirit. May grace guide your journey.

All the best Amit on your first book.

Much love,

Dr Raashi Khatri Panjabi

MD – Orofacial Pain/Headaches and TMJ disorders,
Diplomat of American Board of Orofacial Pain

INTRODUCTION

Hello, my readers! I am sure that you have this book in your hand because you are a seeker. You are in quest for physical, mental, emotional, and spiritual well-being. You would wish for a perfect pill out there to be discovered by you that would take care of your well-being at all levels. Right? Is there a quick hack to this? Is there a week-long short course that one can enrol into and master this art? Is there a -3day seminar? But your guess is bang on! There isn't any shortcut! There are no quick fixes. You need to start looking at yourself in a different light with a whole new perspective.

Some of you might be struggling with all your might and are engulfed in physically deliberating conditions. Some might be struggling emotionally; some might be getting tortured by the rage of their mental dialogues and negative thought process. One could suffer one of these above-mentioned conditions or a combination of these conditions in varying proportions at any point of time. I want to reaffirm and tell you it's 'OK'. This is part of being human! This is life in the dualistic world. The good part is that we can learn from these experiences and grow rather than being stuck in them. If you get stuck in your mental, emotional, and physical patterns, you will succumb deeper into your self-made hellish vortex. You need to take ownership of the circumstances that you are experiencing and learn from them and grow. That is all that we need to do, EVOLVE. It's not that simple, but we have to make an effort, walk the path, and have a clear intent to go on progressing forward. We are nothing but a by-product of millions of years of evolution, and now looks like we, as a human race have hit a plateau. Everyone is focusing on power, fame, wealth, and external happiness. It is time to look inward and start creating internal happiness and achieve clarity. Go within!

My story is the same. I hit a plateau too! And I started

going downhill from there. I was facing a health condition that I could not understand, and this forced me to look deeper into myself, to ask difficult questions, which I was evading. Relooking at my priorities, my lifestyle, my work, my attitude, everything that made me the person I thought I was. Things only started to change when I decided that enough was enough and decided to take control and power back into my own hands. I read a lot, researched, and watched many video podcasts of great spiritual educators. I took up various courses, and equipped myself with tools and skillsets to up the ante. I am still on my journey and I am learning as well as evolving as I write this book. I am sure my journey and the insights that I have gained will resonate with my readers, and I hope that this would help my readers create a more meaningful and happier life.

During my journey, I picked up courses, got certified, did exhaustive research on Nutrition, Physical Health, Mental and Emotional Wellness, Breathing methodologies, Spiritual Practices, and Quantum

Physics. I refrain from calling myself an expert, but I am sure that what I have learned during my journey will go a long way in helping others, and that's the very essence of this book.

There is NO EXCUSE for not doing things that might help you. You are the one in charge, you have always been in charge, and it is time to take things in your hand to create the beautiful LIFE that you have been seeking since forever. No more waiting, procrastinating, NOW is the time to take those actions. There is only NOW, and you exist only in the NOW. So any change that you need to make, has to be done NOW. Empower yourself, create your reality, and live your life fully!

I sincerely hope that you would enjoy reading and learning from this book, just as much as I am excited to share it with you.

WITH LOVE,

AMIT BUTANI

AMNESIA

Chapter 1
EARLY DAYS

I WAS BORN IN THE FINANCE and fashion capital of India, the city of Mumbai, where I presently live. My childhood days of what I remember were spent in India's beautiful capital, New Delhi, since we moved to this city when I was just two years old. My father ran his own business. The business was growing, and it required us, a family of four, including my elder sibling, to relocate there. We lived in New Delhi for almost the entirety of my childhood, eight years before shifting to Mumbai when I was ten years old. We lived in a beautiful neighbourhood called Safdarjung Enclave. I was blessed to have my childhood days growing up there, and I thank the universe for this. It was a beautiful "fairy tale" like neighbourhood with buildings, which encircled a huge oval lush green park.

Having a park for children to play is a boon. You spend most of your playtime in the garden, playing games with friends you befriend at your neighbourhood. You get an excellent physical workout, develop your social skills, lose and win games, understand what team effort is all about, and learn how to deal with defeat. The garden was a great teacher to me! The park was equipped with swings and slides, and various obstacle courses. It was a child's paradise. It was a beautiful place for all of the kids to come together and take part in different sports. Not only for the kids, but their parents also socialized there and discussed everything under the sun from politics to cooking to household problems. Everyone knew everyone in the neighbourhood; it was like one big giant family living in peace and harmony. I always had lots of friends, I felt truly blessed. Even the parents got along well with each other. To top it, most of us even went to the same school! Our school bus stop was a -5 to -7minute walk from our respective houses. We were blessed to have a house help who would take us in the early morning to the school bus stop and fetch us back in the afternoon. I vividly remember the beautiful, innocent conversations that I used to have with friends during the walks to and from the stop.

At that time, fortunately, technology had not taken over yet. I am not against technology. It has its advantages, but I feel grateful that technology did not control our lives back then in hindsight. We used to come back from school by lunchtime, did our school work and went down to play in the park for hours till our parents would call out our names from the balconies of their respective houses to make us come home. That was quite a hilarious sight! We got in a lot of physical activity. We played hockey, cricket, football, Frisbees, swings, and loved going up the slides. It was a merry time for me, full of beautiful moments and lovely friendships.

During my childhood days, I used to watch many movies on my VCR (Video Cassette Recorders), and one of such was Super Snooper starring Terence Hill and Bud Spencer. There were two super cops, and one of them had magical superpowers. Even during that time, when I was very young, I thought I could do the same magic as the guy in the movie. Like holding the glass of water close to my hand and attracting it towards me! Or think of elevating myself off the floor! It was a childish feeling, but deep down, I had this innate knowing that extraordinary things can be a possibility even back then. I just knew it!

Now let me tell about a few out of the ordinary experiences that were inexplicable. Let's begin. The first one was when I was on a swing in my school ground during the recess period, swinging merrily high, oblivious to the commotions around me of other children playing and making merry. While swinging hard at the upswing peak, the swing broke from its hinges, and I was thrown off high into the air and landed on my feet luckily, in a crouched position. But It felt like my legs were pushed hard into my lungs as if crushing it, and I had problem breathing for a few moments. Somewhat I was gasping for air. It felt like my breathing had stopped! Yet throughout this experience existed a feeling of serenity and calm that I experienced. It felt out of the normal! I didn't inform anyone about this incident and kept to myself. Fortunately, there weren't any physical injuries.

The next experience soon followed. We used to play hand-cricket (wherein we use our hand as a cricket bat for hitting the ball) in my school's senior assembly area, which was situated outdoors. I remember the rules of this variation of the game where one was allowed to catch the ball with one hand after the ball bounced once on the floor, and it was considered as the batsmen is out, i.e., he has lost his wicket. Yeah, own turf, own home rules! The batsmen, a friend of mine, hit the ball high, and I ran after it to catch it. It bounced off the floor once, and after the bounce, I caught it, but guess what! In the enthusiasm of running after the ball and catching it after the bounce, I had not realized that I had come right up to the edge of the assembly area. At the end of the assembly area, there was a significant drop from the edge, and underneath were rocks and stones and wild green grass growing. So I reached for the ball with one hand to catch it, and then I realized that it's too late to hold back, and I am going to fall off the edge! I shut my eyes tightly, and in a blink, just a matter of milliseconds, I was on the floor on my soft, comfy bum and was not hurt! Not only that, I fell away from the rocks which could have caused me some severe physical damage or even head injury. As if it was magic! Nothing had happened, and no damage was done. In hindsight, it feels as if I was guided mysteriously by some higher intelligence that protected me. After that, of course, like any other young kid of my age, I fought with my friends, insisting that the batsman was out, but no one listened to me because technically I caught the ball and passed over the boundary fence. It was a typical innocent child-like fight over a lost cause with my friends; I soon forgot about this incident though. But to this day, this episode remains etched in my heart.

The third and the most profound experience I had happened during Diwali (a widely celebrated Hindu festivity). "Diwali is the Indian festival of lights, usually lasting five days and celebrated during the Hindu Lunisolar month Kartika. One of the most popular festivals of Hinduism, Diwali symbolizes the spiritual victory of light over darkness, good over evil, and knowledge over ignorance." The incident took place during the nighttime. My sister, who is older by three years, and I mostly slept in our parents' room. On most occasions, I would land sleeping in between my parents on the same bed while my sister used to sleep on the floor on a mattress. Some of us get the privileges of being the younger pampered one in the family. That particular night while I was sleeping between them, I was awakened for some reason. I looked up, and I saw an older man looking at me and speaking something or gesticulating to someone dressed in a traditional outfit (which I think now was Manali/Nepali traditional wear). He was smiling while talking to someone. When I looked behind him, I saw a female, who I thought was his wife. She was wearing the same traditional wear. It was not a dream and felt extremely real, and I could sense this from my core of being. I froze in fear and did not have the guts to speak. I didn't even have the courage to wake up my mother. I shut my eyes tightly and opened again, and they both were still there! Although when I saw them, somehow I didn't feel threatened by their presence. It was more of a benign presence. I must have shut and opened my eyes quite a few times, and finally when I opened my eyes one of the times, they were gone! Puff! Into the cold night air!

I got up from the bed to see and didn't see anyone in the darkness. This was a surreal experience, and I, for the first time, experienced something beyond my five senses' perception. It was beyond what the human mind could comprehend, and thus I knew I had experienced this magical phenomenon! These were the early signs which showed me that such occurrences, which not everyone can perceive or experience, had some learning for me in store and took me on a path that made me pursue what I have set for myself to do in this lifetime. At that time, I must have been 8 or 9 years old. Although these experiences had a profound impact on me, I did not think much of it then. Little did I realize that the universe was setting up my ordained path.

Chapter 2
THE SIGNS

AFTER STAYING IN NEW DELHI for eight years, I was informed by my mother about relocating back to our house in Mumbai, India, where I was born. It was quite overwhelming for an almost -10year-old to be uprooted from his beautiful neighbourhood, childhood friends, and school friends. It was heart-wrenching to say goodbye to your friends and relatives, but there was no way out seemingly. Change is the only constant in life, they say, but there was despair in the heart and hopelessness in the air. The feeling of the void was indescribable. This concluded my early childhood phase. We could not afford plane tickets in those times, so we took an intercity train from Delhi to Mumbai. The journey used to take approximately 18 hours. All of us took this train journey excluding my father, as he had to drive down to Mumbai by the car we owned! The train journey was tormenting, as leaving New Delhi was emotional for all of us.

Take 2. Circa Mumbai 1987, I am 10 years old. Everything is new to me, new friends, new school, new neighbourhood, and a new phase of my life. I was still reeling from the emotional upheaval of leaving New Delhi and my childhood friends behind. Now an adventure in another city laid before me. I thought no looking back now, and I decided that I might as well experience this new phase with zest and complete involvement. You always have a choice. That's free will, right? Although there was a feeling of being uprooted and losing a sense of being centred, I gradually started settling into my new life in Mumbai. I made new friends in my school and neighbourhood. Evenings were fun-filled with games like four corners, hide n' seek, street cricket etc. Mumbai being like any other big bustling city in the world, there was a lack of open spaces. We used to play cricket in the streets on Sundays, something new to me at that time!

Luckily my father was a member of a sporting club close by home, and there I used to go swimming regularly and eventually started my competitive swimming career. I also used to play squash and do other sporting activities. It was a boon for people living in a city like Mumbai, where not plenty of open spaces were available. I finished school and started my junior college life. I was pursuing science as I wanted to pursue engineering. The choices were so limited back then you could either pursue arts, commerce, or science as your base and then graduate either as an Engineer or as a Doctor. I chose the former.

While I pursued science, I got another push towards my calling, my path. I found immense pleasure in reading nonfictional books. I started reading various books. It had a lot to do with spirituality, science, healing, and health. Some of the exciting reads were the DANCING WU LU MASTERS, MANY LIVES MANY MASTERS, LAWS OF THE SPIRIT WORLD, and CONVERSATIONS WTH GOD. The list was endless. I have put a reference for a list of books for further readings and research at the end. I got attracted towards meditation, positive affirmations, and visualizations. I have a friend who was on the same journey, and I remember we used to discuss many of these topics back then. None of our other friends could relate to this, and during those times, these subjects were not widely spoken of as they are today.

My first experience with the law of attraction came soon during my junior college days before I went into engineering. I always visualized a girlfriend for me, someone about 5 feet, 6 inches, mid-level shoulder level length hair, attractive, fair complexioned, and good-natured. This person would eventually become my life partner. I had made a note of this in my note book! Lo, behold! Soon in a couple of months after that, I met the love of my life, with whom I am happily married to now with two beautiful kids. I didn't realize it at that time when I started dating her, but soon after a couple of months, I was jolted in my boots when I opened the diary where I had written a description of hers, and I was like WOW, this stuff actually works! We started dating and got involved with each other at a deeper emotional level, and right there, and I knew that we were meant to get married.

I was fascinated also about having out-of-body experiences (OBE) and researching how to have them during these days. I was intrigued by this idea, and nowhere had I even doubted that this could not be possible! By this time, I was in my teens, pursuing engineering, and at that time I used to be raw, open-minded, and not so conditioned by societal beliefs, and open to new ideas and adventures; I was getting more attracted towards spirituality and meditation and having an OBE.

I had my first OBE while I was in the second or first year of engineering college. I was practicing these exercises for OBE, wherein you get into a dream state, and you realize it's a dream and start controlling it and then finally wake up from the trance consciously. I tried these exercises for a couple of weeks, and Voila, it happened! Unexpectedly one fine morning, I was asleep and had a dream, and I was conscious that I am in a dream, and I shook myself and woke up from the dream. I felt light like a feather, lifting upwards, towards my room's ceiling, and I remember clearly going through the ceiling, to my terrace and consciously pulling myself downwards. I could then sense the room's ceiling fan, the blades of which were going through me! I could see my room, and I watched the room lit up with not my physical eyes but spiritual eyes, and it was early morning. I saw my bedroom cupboards in front of me in all its detail with posters and stickers put on them, and then slowly, I moved my attention towards the sliding door of the room, which was shut. I remembered looking at the door and the bright golden yellowish doorknob and thinking, how do I get past this?

Even in this avatar, I can say that I possessed or controlled my mind, but I was not the mind. I was deliberating how I would go past the door to the other side. There was an inbuilt intuition that I could perform this, so I just passed slowly through the door with just the thought of moving! While passing through the door, I had this fantastic, sensational experience in my spiritual self. This feeling of joy was tremendous! I was now in my house passage, and I was staring at my living room straight ahead. I just thought, and in a blink of light, I was through my living room window and straight onto the pavement right outside my house, diagonally opposite my house! Then in a matter of milliseconds, I was sucked right back into my physical body, and my physical eyes opened. It felt like being rocked in my body. It was abrupt!

I was back in my room, it was early in the morning. I know in my heart that this was not a dream. Something beyond the ordinary had transpired. I had explored and ventured out beyond my five senses' perception. To date, even after 25 odd years, I remember this incident so vividly as if it happened a moment ago! After this fantastic experience for a couple of weeks, I felt invincible. It felt why do I stress about life so much. Why are people not enjoying their lives? We all live forever beyond the physical! Our true self cannot be destroyed. It was an amazing feeling! Another OBE incident soon followed this while I watched television, and I reached a lucid state and felt I was flying through clouds and over continents! I could feel the sensation of breeze and zipping at a high speed. I was sucked back down to the physical body then. I guess my spiritual body was becoming loose and being able to easily detach from my physical body. But soon, engineering and the rigmaroles of physical life took over, and I was sucked back right into the mundane flow of Human existence.

I continued my practice of meditations and affirmations, and continued devouring books. Some of them were gems like AUBIOGRAPHY OF THE YOGI, I AM THAT, YOU ARE THE PLACEBO, and practiced visualizations methods whenever time could permit. I had now started working after graduating from Engineering but then decided to pursue Post Graduation. I wanted to do my MBA, live outside the comfort of my familiar surroundings. I wanted to pursue my post-graduate degree course outside the country. I wanted to challenge myself to be able to survive in a new environment. I felt it was necessary and part of my evolution. Thus I went on to pursue my MBA in the UK. Now you will see again that without an iota of doubt the law of attraction working also in this case. I had always visualized that one of my close friends will come along with me from Mumbai to pursue the MBA course. The wish was placed with the universe, and then it finally happened. I was going for a drive late in the evening in Mumbai's streets, months before I was scheduled to leave. Probably during this time I happened to bump into a friend of mine who was at a corner stall, buying some household products. I was having a casual conversation with him, and I happened to tell him about my plan to study MBA abroad. I got a call the very next day, and he mentioned doing about this course with me! I went on to use the law of attraction and visualized my MBA program schooling, and it all went precisely in the same way as envisioned. The first semester was the toughest, and I was one of the few that sailed through. I had terrific lodging and boarding at the prime locale of London "thanks to my aunt". The MBA and London days taught me a lot. This experience was a great teacher.

I learned to stay completely on my own and got my degree with honour. I visited various cities in Europe, and made new friends. The law of attraction worked seamlessly. I wasn't meditating enough, but I was doing a lot of visualizations which were working! When you visualize, you need to consider the outcome to be an absolute deal without resistance. Believe it and live the end result and then sit back and allow the universe to respond to your request and let the answers come to you eventually. Don't get involved in the details on how to achieve the outcome. Just feel the result and leave the planning and details to the grand and infinite intelligence of the universe.

I finished my program in the UK and returned to India, and after that soon got married to my childhood sweetheart. My next tryst with the law of attraction came when we were trying to start a family. I always visualized that I would have a boy and a girl. My wife was not ready to start a family as we both used to love to travel. Finally, 5 to 6 years into marriage, both side parents (typical becoming of Indian parents) were pushing us so much that we finally decided to start a family. At this point, I started visualizing my wife with a cute tummy bump and walking out of our bedroom bathroom, holding her back, and treading along slowly. I always expressed gratitude and a feeling of appreciation whenever I saw a pregnant lady or child with her mother on the street. Expressing gratitude to the universe for desires that we want automatically pulls those desires and wants towards us faster. I visualized the pregnancy with great detail. Very soon when we were both on yet another travel escapade of ours to Northern India, we realized that my wife had conceived, and she was 4 to 6 weeks pregnant!. This was another wonderful confirmation to me that revealed that the law of attraction works every single time! Not only this, within two years, we got another baby, and my wife played a prank with my mother and said that we are expecting another baby girl. I was confident that it's not possible as I have visualized a baby boy. I had pictured toasting with my friends on having a boy and sending a text message to all of them when the baby boy was delivered. I even visualized the text message that I would send! This visualization, like all others, was very detailed. I soon caught my wife's prank, and we were getting a baby boy! The universe, like a genie, once again answered my prayers.

Somehow I always felt that Universe was looking out for me. When my job was not going that great, I believed that something more magical and awesomeness awaited me. I remember thinking about what new exciting possibilities awaits me, and then suddenly, out of nowhere, I got an opportunity to work in a travel retail company in Dubai, UAE, along with my family that too with an attractive package! I was being pulled out from the hard core engineering business to a travel retail business, which I knew nothing about. A different Industry, a fun, and lively industry, and in an adventurous and lovely city of Dubai. My wife was incredibly supportive, without which I could never have had the courage to move on. My parents were also supportive of this decision. We got this opportunity in December

2011, In Feb 2012, we were in Dubai!. Thank you, Universe!

It was once again time for new beginnings, and leaving your loved ones and family behind is never comfortable. But for something new to happen in your life, the old must pass on. All of us felt emotional, leaving the vibrant city of Mumbai, but at the same time we were looking forward to our new phase as a family of four in the desert city of Dubai, UAE!

Chapter 3
THE FINAL BLOW

HERE I AM IN THE desert land, a place of fast cars, best architectures, amazing landscape, and the hospitable sheikhs. Dubai is such a beautiful city with a potpourri of international culture. My wife and I came a few weeks before I started my new job, so that we can find a place to stay, and we zeroed it in a beautiful neighbourhood. I shifted there soon after, and my wife along with our kids followed shortly after securing school admissions for the kids. The flat and the community we selected were perfect, spacious apartments in an impressive residential complex in Downtown Dubai. The best ambiance for our kids to grow up and play. The complex was self-sustained. It had numerous multi-cuisine restaurants, cafes, bars, chemists, hospitals, barbershops, grocery stores; a fully functional gym, yoga house with fitness trainers; swimming pools, health club, Jacuzzi, sauna, you name any facility, it has high chances of being there.

Several parks were situated on the podium level and ground level for kids to play in. There was a 1 KM jogging track running around the park. Above all, we were blessed to have a great landlord who gave us the apartment with almost ready to move in furniture and fixtures. Moving in was the only thing left! Once again, immense gratitude to the universe. I had a great job, wherein I was the VP of a new business vertical, which the company was building from scratch. It was exciting and, at the same time, challenging and stressful. I had to prove myself in the organization, and I ensured that I left no stone unturned!

Starting a new strategic business unit for the company was an amazing opportunity but also demanding. To top it off, you have a boss who has a fine eye for details and pushes you hard to juice you to your maximum potential. There were unending presentations to new investors who wanted to invest in the company, which was still growing. A lot of international travel was involved. Office working hours were very early, and I often had to meet frequent deadlines. Materialistic possession and aspirations, drive to impress superiors; proving my work to others; being always available to my superiors; recognition, and approval from others became my mantra. At the same time, I started pushing myself physically very hard to keep up with my rigid health regime supplemented with not so good eating habits that took a heavy toll on me emotionally and physically. I did not realize that I was pushing myself hard, and I never opened up to my family as I didn't want them to feel the stress that I was going through. Still, at the same time, I could feel that a chaotic internal eruption was taking place and eating me from within. I always thought I could not get stressed out and had a fantastic ability to handle pressure and perform well, but guess I was wrong! I had to fit in my workout routine with these crazy work schedules and deadlines, because physical exercise had become part of my daily routine since childhood because of my competitive swimming days. I also had no time left for meditation and visualizing techniques. I was losing a grip on my spiritual self! I was juggling between stressful work, pressure on meeting deadlines, exhausting physical workout, family life, and on top of it, not so well eating and drinking habits. With this lifestyle, the inevitable was waiting to happen!

Here, I would like to mention that we explored UAE to its hilt and left no opportunity to explore this wonderful country with all its interesting attractions.

Our friends in the UAE used to say that we have explored so much in a short period that we spent in UAE, typically than what most people do in 20 years! We used to drive down to Oman for short vacations occasionally. My tryst with health happened when we were back from our Muscat's family trip in October 2014. We were visiting our friends who we had befriended during our stay in the UAE, and to date, we are very much in touch and connected. During this Muscat trip, like always, we had a fantastic time. I had to report to work the next morning, so we drove back the day before in the evening. Dubai to Muscat is a good 5 to 6 hours' drive but a pleasurable one.

We got back late in the evening, and before leaving for work early morning the next day, I went out for a quick run in the park, came back, showered, and left for work. I started feeling uneasy around lunchtime. I clearly remember I had packed for myself a subway from the food court close by to work and started to eat my lunch when I felt though

I was sinking and felt a sense of disequilibrium. I was trying to put my head down for another bite, and I felt that I was falling internally and could not hold myself. It felt like an internal rocking motion that one could not see for someone looking at me. I informed this condition to my colleague, who took me swiftly to the local clinic close by, and they checked me for my sugar and BP, and all was OK. I remember even feeling shaky at the clinic in the chair I was sitting in. It felt terrible. My colleague, who was such a Good Samaritan, had been with me throughout this ordeal. I can never thank him enough!

Meanwhile, I could not explain this sense of disequilibrium I felt and could not convey it either. We came back from the clinic, and the biggest mistake I made is I went in that very evening trampoline jumping with my friends, ignoring what had happened during the day. I guess this outing only aggravated my condition!

I was supposed to travel to the Philippines in a

couple of days because of work, but I could not as I was not feeling well. This condition was not like vertigo but a sense of disequilibrium, a feeling of not being in control. No one could understand this, and I was in a helpless situation. As days passed, there was disequilibrium now accompanied by various painful sensations moving over my foreheads in multiple places. My eyes used to get irritated by light and the sun. The disequilibrium feeling would continue; I would get tingling sensations all over my face and sometimes painful sensations accompanied by tingling going down towards my feet. I was experiencing unpleasant sensations all over my body. This became a deliberating condition in a matter of days!

I started to lose my confidence, I could not even drive to work, and I needed my wife around all the time. I was under the constant grip of fear of fainting all of a sudden! The worst part of this was that no one could understand my dilemma. Physically from the outside, everything looked normal to everyone.

Everyone said that it's stress, even now that I think about it I think it might have played a significant role, but there was a lot more going on. I asked the UNIVERSE or GOD what is happening to me. Why is this happening to me? What did I do to deserve this? I had lost all hope!

THE METAMORPHOSIS

Chapter 4
HITTING LOW

IN A MATTER OF SHORT time, I had become a complete nervous wreck. I wanted to find answers, dive deep within the core of my being, and realize what's happening to my body. I wanted to go to the root cause of all these. I was agitated. I was constantly in a state of worry and anxiety. How could a fit person like myself suffer this ordeal, the dilemma was if I could not accept it, or I would not accept it!

I went to my neighbourhood doctor in the complex where we were staying. After explaining my condition, examining me, and after some blood work, he informed me that I have Polycythaemia. It's a blood condition in which you need to keep the "RBC" in check by donating blood for the rest of your life, and that's the only solution you have. I am sure the doctor meant well, but I was quite concerned. The stupidest thing I did is research the condition on Google, and I concluded that this would be the end of my world!. I got more hassled. I went the very next day and donated blood. I felt good during that day, but still, this condition persisted! Maybe it was a placebo effect. I was subscribed to medication. After not finding relief, I sought an ENT specialist's help to see if anything was wrong with my inner ear, my hearing, as it relates to balancing the body. I undertook some tests for hearing as I read somewhere; if there is a problem with the internal ear, it could lead to disequilibrium. The results of the tests were satisfactory. Then shortly I got my sonography done to see if all the internal organs were functioning fine. I even met a diabetologist who did a blood test for sugar fasting levels, checking for hyperglycaemia. All results came back normal.

I went to another ENT specialist for a second opinion, who prescribed me medicines for vertigo, which I started taking. I went through ECG to check for an irregular heartbeat. I was even given a heart altimeter, which I had to wear taped on my chest for two days.! The readings for all came out normal. I tested my blood from various path labs, as suggested by doctors, Nada! Nothing, all reports were standard! One day at work, I felt I was fainting and panicked! I think it was nothing but a panic attack triggered by my condition, and I was an emotional wreck in all ways. I got myself admitted to a hospital. I did an MRI of the head, neck, and brain stem region done. The MRI was one and a half-hour of painful moments inside a machine. It can cause extreme claustrophobia for those who have not undergone an MRI, if they are suffering from anxiety from closed spaces. The loud noise, the high pitched sound of the machine was definitely not music to my ears. Yet I conditioned myself to remain calm during the entire process. Years of practicing meditations and focussing on my breath did come in handy. After looking at the report, the doctor diagnosed that I have peripheral vertigo. I was again prescribed drugs and strong steroid medicines. I even went to a neurophysician to see if I felt sensations on my feet and face. All tests again came back normal. These numerous visits to the doctors and tests cost me a lot, but thank God for insurance!

During all these months of visiting doctors, specialists, clinics, and health practitioners, I got well-versed in all the medical terms and its nuances, not even joking! There was a sense of sliding into a vortex of self-destruction.

Then in between, we came to India during our children's school break. The saga of doctor-visits continued as I visited a chiropractor, who supposedly realigned my neck during several visits and got me started on homeopathy medication for the same. During my stay in India, I also did my CT angiography to see if all the blood vessels of the heart into the cranium section and lower body worked fine. Plus, some more blood work and tests. I was getting drained by all this, and at the same time, exasperated for not being able to find answers, or solutions. I was emotionally, physically, and mentally shattered.

When we were back in Dubai, I continued experiencing my symptoms. I had to sit through office meetings, board presentations, and investor meets while experiencing debilitating conditions, painful sensations, and the rocking and disequilibrium feeling. It was a tormenting phase of my life. I remember once in a Dubai hospital; my wife was in tears to see me this way as she always saw me as a happy-go-lucky kind of a person, a healthy individual, who used to love working out and keep himself fit. Seeing me helpless on the bed, I guess she could not control her tears. We both had some intensely emotional moments during this phase. I drowned in self-pity. Not being able to drive, be independent, always living in fear, and became dependent, I resided in the fact that there was no way out. I guess this is the lowest point that I had hit in my life!

Guess, once you hit the lowest low, then the only way is up! I remember one of my friends in Mumbai mentioning to me that there is a pain specialist for the shoulder and above the region, in Mumbai, who coincidently happens to be my friend's sister! Without the slightest of hesitation, I explained my condition-and-experiences to her and the various tests that I had undertaken. She only asked for an X-ray of my head and neck region. Within a day, she diagnosed it and said it's a forward head syndrome because of staying long time on the office desk with drooping shoulders. The lower head posture has got a lot to do with this condition, and running with this condition only aggravated it! She informed me that there is no loss of hope, and we need to work on this with a physiotherapist, and prescribed me some muscle relaxants, pain meds to help this condition. I just hit an epiphany moment! What she diagnosed somehow resonated well within. She was like an Angel sent from up above in my dire need of assistance in this situation of distress!

It's said that once you are prepared to take on responsibility and take power in your hand, the universe organizes itself to support you.

I guess the time had come to RECLAIM MY POWER!

Chapter 5
TAKING CHARGE

LIKE A RISING PHOENIX FROM the ashes, I was ready to take on the path of empowerment. Reclaiming my mastery and equipping myself with all possible knowledge and learnings to understand my own self and my self-worth. As I was wallowing in self-pity, fear, doubt, the victim-syndrome, I made a decision finally enough was enough! There has to be more to this! I can't keep living like this, I thought to myself. I had to be strong. I have to face my terrors and qualms and come out triumphant! I had to be strong for my wife, my kids, and my parents. My parents were going through emotional turmoil in Mumbai, India, and they felt helpless. I am grateful to God that I had my family backing me up during my rough phase. I looked at my past experiences as learning, like the universe has taught me a lesson, as a grand teacher, and I came to realize soon enough THE NEED to move beyond these circumstances and conquer my emotions, doubts, fears, and focus only on positives, strength, hope. Change the way you think, feel, and act, and you change your life. That's it!

Having said the above, I realized that it was not going to be an easy task. I had become a slave of my old habit, the same patterns of thinking, feeling, and behaving. I was recreating the same thoughts and emotions every day. I had become a prisoner of my thinking. It was tough! There were days when I felt lost, weak, and disempowered, but then there were days I felt strong and realized that any situation could be overpowered and mastered. It was a roller coaster ride. I was in a state of flux. There were days of highs-and-lows. It was an internal fight between my inner good and evil. It just depended on who I was feeding my energies. I was going through a drastic change and but this had to be done. Let me tell you that any change that needs to take place should come from within. ONE NEEDS TO TAKE THE CHARGE. It was my internal battle, and I was going to fight it alone. I had to overcome my self-imposed limitations.

The knowledge needs to set in deep into the core of your heart that whatever is happening to you in your life is yours and only your responsibility! A tough pill to digest, huh? You need to take ownership of all that is happening to you, the emotions that you are going through, the thoughts you are attracting, and the amount of energy that was being given to the external situation that you are experiencing. Everything is your creation! You are the master creator of your life, and no one else! It is difficult to accept, but when one stops complaining and playing the victim card and starts taking responsibilities, there comes a feeling of power, charge, and control. Then arises the desire for living in full awareness and consciousness. We all live most of our lives in our heads, inside our minds, and that itself is a place filled with traces of fear and self-doubt and disempowerment for the majority of the people. One needs to start living fully in the moment now.

Now is the only moment what we always had and always will have. There is no other moment when you will have the control in your hand. If you think of anything fearful that happened to you in the past, you are thinking about it now. If you are procrastinating about the future and getting anxious, you are doing the now moment. Live in the NOW. You cannot have thoughts in the NOW, about the NOW, as you are living it. Being in the NOW with no over-thinking is a beautiful experience. More energy is available to you while living the NOW than thinking in vain. Focus more, intensity into your action, and a sense of flow and ease can be experienced when not living in the future or the past.

I realized I had to start changing and moulding myself on all levels. I had to change my mental and emotional state. I had to start operating from a better mental and emotional reference level. I soon began to realize that creation first begins inside your mind. Start being conscious of the thoughts, be an observer to them, and do not get entangled. A side note here, it's NOT EASY at all. You cannot help but get sucked into your thoughts. You might feel you own them. They are yours. It's challenging to let go! But I had to make a conscious effort to direct my mind towards positive thoughts, in order to use thoughts for positive creation and not get entangled with unnecessary chattering of the mind. Thoughts do become things as thoughts attract like vibrations, and they manifest eventually. That's your creative power. But at the same time, stop living only in your thoughts and start living life! Don't believe blindly in every thought of yours. Give energy to your thoughts, which you want to manifest in your life for your well-being. Positive thoughts will lead to positive emotions, and thus to your well-being.

I also had to take responsibility for my physical health. We all remember the phrase from school - "a healthy mind in a healthy body." I couldn't have learned it in a better way. I had to be conscious of what I am putting inside my body. I realized how much abuse I had caused to this body, the temple of the living God. Far too much overconsumption of alcohol, junk food, wrong eating times, and bad food choices had made me come to this point. The wrong sleeping schedule happened because of crazy work hours which was immensely damaging to my health. I have always been a fitness enthusiast, but I had to be aware of when I pushed myself too hard. I was overstretching my body. I was addicted to exercising, but my body was breaking down due to lack of proper nutrition and sleep, and I didn't realize it. Maybe this was also one of the reasons behind my experience.

There was a feeling of experiencing something beyond life's duality, an awareness that knew everything but was not affected by the earthly happenings around. During my crazy work hours in Dubai, I had completely ignored my spiritual growth. I was not meditating. I wasn't practicing visualizations and manifestation methodologies. I was not spending time alone in silence. I was ignoring myself. I was always looking outwards for completion and fulfilment and not going inwards to search for answers. I was concerned more about my external situation and had no clue about the inner turmoil taking place, which lead to my suffering.

I had to start looking at my well-being at a holistic level. That is at a physical, mental and emotional, and spiritual level. It became my Mantra!

Time to take charge but with full awareness that I will be bound to hit roadblocks, I will experience ups and downs, but now the choice to empower myself and rise above my self-created demons, self-doubt, misery and to rise above it had been cemented inside me. The power to change than to remain in this situation was way higher. I had to be back on my ground, be active, get fit, and live a joyous and fulfilling life. It is always NOW when we make a choice, and I had made mine! It was time to SIMPLIFY LIVING.

Chapter 6
LEARNING FROM THE TEACHERS

NOW THE PARADIGM SHIFT HAD started. A new pathway was set in motion. I had decided to take things into my hands now and decided the end of external circumstances dictating my life. It was time to operate from an internal locus of control. The devil and the Satan are within every one of us and depend entirely upon who we nurse. Writing this book has made me dwell deeper into my experiences and enabled me to learn from them. It has been extremely therapeutic for me. Once you start taking responsibility of your own life and your experiences, this is when things start getting more evident. At the same time, you are faced with extreme challenges, and you begin visiting dark places within the core of your being and healing the untreated wounds.

The internal instability was overwhelming at the time. But even a caterpillar goes through metamorphosis before it transmogrify into a butterfly. One goes through this process to achieve a breakthrough on the other side. It is inevitable. The learning needs to be permanent and permeable at all levels of your existence. The universe is a harsh taskmaster, and you have to be a good student and get yourself ready to face the tough quest that life has to offer. These analogies are coming from within my heart as I am writing this, and it is incredible when you confront your fears and inner demons and you come to realize that most of them are self-created fallacies. It's so easy to understand, but so difficult to put into practice. Knowledge is good, but if you don't apply and gain wisdom through application, it's futile. One will never grow. I learned it the hard way and am still learning. I guess, that is life, where one is trying to become the next grandest version of oneself. It is all about moments and memories in the end. So let us create a good one!

Now coming back to this phase, where I was looking for a way up from the clutches of darkness and my self-imposed limitations and self-created fears, I started doing extensive research. When the student is ready, the masters or teachers come in various forms to teach you. I decided first that I need to be conscious of my physical health and well-being. I started to become aware of what I was feeding my body. The body is the most gloriously accurate instrument in the Universe, a highly intricate system, and transcendentally beautiful. It is the temple of the soul. I started researching on nutrition, supplements, and minerals requirements for the body. It's ability to repair and regenerate. It's capacity to self-heal. I started avoiding certain foods in my diet. I realized physical exercise is essential. The body is meant for movement. I started once again going for my daily walks, albeit strolling. During my walks, I started listening to a whole lot of podcasts on nutrition and well-being. I started listening to scientific information on holistic well-being.

My first teachers came as a video experience on a YouTube channel. His name was Bruce Lipton. He has written an excellent book called the biology of belief. In 1982, Dr. Lipton began examining the principles of quantum physics and how they might be integrated into his understanding of the cell's information processing systems. "He produced breakthrough studies on the cell membrane, which revealed that this outer layer of the cell was an organic homologue of a computer chip, the cell's equivalent of a brain. His research at Stanford University's School of Medicine, between 1987 and

1992, revealed that the environment, operating through the membrane, controlled the behaviour and physiology of the cell, turning genes on and off. His discoveries, which ran counter to the established scientific view that life is controlled by the genes, presaged one of today's most important fields of study, the science of epigenetics." In this, Bruce speaks about epigenetics and clearly states that %90 of our diseases happen not through genes but due to the environment in which cells grow.[1] The body chemistry affects the well-being of our cells. We are a body of trillions of cells and bacteria colonies on how our moods and beliefs make up our bodies' chemistry. There exists a strong connection between the mind and body! How changing your beliefs can change your body functions and keep it in optimal health.

Then came another great teacher, Wayne Dyer. He was a beautiful teacher, and I loved his blogs and meditations. He has written many books. His

[1]https://www.brucelipton.com/about

famous words were, "I AM that I AM", and one of his fantastic books is *Change Your Thoughts, and You Change Your Life*. His lectures were profound and resonated with me deeply. I remember listening to all his podcasts which helped me in achieving inner balance and helped me to get focused.

I encountered soon after that and was influenced by a young Spiritual entrepreneur Sandeep Maheshwari. He spoke about his journey. His presentations and videos were on mind, mind control, emotions, and many other subjects. I also heard about his journey from Vipassana and how it changed him from inside out.

So l, from there, I got attracted to Vipassana teaching. Shri S. N. Goenka had ten videos in English for ten days of Vipassana, which my father shared, and I used to listen to one video every night. I was enthralled and fascinated by the exposure to such teachings, which I knew nothing about. Vipassana is gentle but at the same time a tough and thorough technique of meditation. "According to dhamma.

org, it is an observation-based, self-exploratory journey that focuses on the deep interconnection between the mind and body, which is realized through disciplined attention to the physical sensations."[2]

I started my meditations regularly and staying centred within. From there, I began to read and watch more videos relating to spirituality posted by Deepak Chopra. I liked his book- "Life After Death". Then I went on to see the video tubes of Mooji. I went on to read a fantastic book from Anita Moorjani called "Dying To Be Me". "After her cancer diagnosis in 2002, Moorjani was taken to a hospital in 2006, where she lay in a coma for 30 hours, during which Moorjani claims to have undergone a Near Death Experience,[3] which changed her life. I was fortunate to have read this book." Then eventually came on other great teachers into my life, Rupert Spira, then

[2] https://www.indiatoday.in/lifestyle/health/story/what-exactly-is-vipassana-the-meditation-technique-president-kovind-swears-by-1145720-2018-01-15

[3] Wikipedia

Dr. Joe Dispenza, whose book – "You Are The Placebo", is a fantastic read. More enlightened souls kept coming into my reality as if I were attracting them. There were more to follow, Sadguru, Abraham Hicks, Alan Watts, the list goes on and on.

I was fortunate to have read this fantastic book titled I AM THAT by Nisargadatta Maharaj, one of the BEST books that I have encountered exploring and realizing the self. This book is one of the most powerful books out there and a must-read. It is simple in your face and talks about techniques for realizing the self. Then read Autobiography of a Yogi written by Parmahansa Yogananda. This book also had a profound effect on me. In the end, there are references to the books listed that helped me sail through the dark phases of my life and help uplift my mood, spirit, and energy. I thank these teachers from the bottom of my heart for introducing to my life to help in gaining knowledge and wisdom and arrive at this place that I am right now to share my learnings and experiences with all my readers.

Knowledge is useless unless put into application. Just reading is not enough, you need to apply as well! The application of knowledge is called wisdom that will help you to evolve. Transformation work needs to be carried out just knowing what the current habits are not useful.

I realized soon enough that I was getting attracted more and more towards spirituality, science, nutrition, emotional and mental health. I didn't know why, but I felt a strong surge and attraction towards this field. As if to realize that this is where my passion and joy reside.

I think the relationships in my life have been great teachers. I realized that one of my greatest teachers was my boss in Dubai. He was a harsh taskmaster and result oriented. I was always under tremendous pressure from him, and I could not speak up my mind in front of him. It felt as if I was taken for granted, squeezed out. At the same time, I must admit that I had a lot of liberty to make decisions and was exposed to a lot of learning on the work front. I travelled worldwide, increased my networking abilities, formed my own progressive sales team reporting to me, and learned the tricks and business traits.

I am thankful to him for teaching me this, but at that point, I did not realize. I felt extreme pressure during the time. Then it happened one day while I was sitting in my boss's cabin. There was a heated discussion going on, and there was this inner calling, which said, "NOW it is ENOUGH!." I expressed myself quite vehemently and walked out of the cabin and later in the evening messaged that, If I was not up to the mark, I will gladly step out of the job and quit. I think this was a significant turning point in my life!

I felt I had regained my voice! I expressed it! I could not let these emotions just well up within me as it was done in the past. I vented out, I spoke my heart out, and I voiced. There was a massive sigh of relief as if a gigantic burden was lifted off my chest. It felt good. Luckily for me, the boss became aligned with my thought process and working style, and things fell automatically into place. It was like I had rearranged my internal energies, and everything externally got aligned accordingly. During the course of the next two years, I got shifted to another excellent project, an online e-commerce business model for UAE. It was exciting meeting new vendors, setting up a business from the bottom up. Energies had shifted, and so did my circumstances.

Soon after this, I had an opportunity to shift back to Mumbai, India, after spending five beautiful years in Dubai. I discussed it with my family, and my wife, always being the pillar of my strength, was very supportive of the relocation. The job was heading marketing for the entire India operations of the same Dubai based travel retail organization. It was an excellent upgrade in my designation profile, and we were finally moving back to our home where I was born, and both of us would be back in the city where our parents and extended family resides. Our parents were getting older, and I was sure they would enjoy spending time with their grandkids and us. So we moved back to Mumbai and our friends, it was a great feeling. Meanwhile, my spiritual sojourn was getting more and more intense.

On moving back to Mumbai, I had the beautiful experience of being introduced to the teachings of Meher Baba, who has a pilgrimage centred in Meherabad, Ahmednagar, a 6 hour drive from Mumbai. The place is serene and oozes peace and tranquillity. The energies of the place are overwhelming. The preaching of Meher Baba is SILENCE; that's it! There was a quote at his tomb at the pilgrimage centre which read 'All things real and true are taught in Silence'. His teachings and energy of the place just threw me head on to my spiritual quest. He still is a great teacher in my life. Though I could never relate to the physical aspect of Meher Baba, I could relate to him in terms of higher energy and frequency.

I got introduced to the work of Ramana Maharshi and had a fantastic opportunity to visit his ashram in Tiruvannamalai. I got acquainted with the work of Robert Adams as well, another great teacher. Everything had now started pointing inwards. I started meditating more, doing self-inquiry, healing my past through past life regressing sessions, and visiting a very well-known medium channeller. I started updating myself with courses that were exciting and relating to Energy healing. The teachers were coming into my life and pointing me to my path. The universe speaks in signs, and we need to be conscious to be able to see them. I felt intuitive, I was on the right path, and my teachers had led me to this.

APPLICATION
OF KNOWLEDGE

Chapter 7
PHYSICAL HEALTH

I HAD STARTED TO EQUIP myself with all the knowledge I had gained and started applying them to my daily life and seeing miraculous results. I know our body was meant to heal, but we also need to provide it the right nutrition and the environment.

In this and the following chapters, let me provide you with some tools you could use in your daily lives. In this chapter, let us talk about physical health. What is the definition of physical health? As per certain clinical description, it means when the body is disease-free, and it can operate at optimal fitness level. Regular exercise, nutrition, sleep, and cutting down on junk food are vital to retain physical health.

Let us first discuss physical exercise and movement. Your body is designed not to be stationery but to be in a state of activity during the day. We are mostly living a sedentary lifestyle. People are most of the time on their handheld devices. Press a button and get your shopping needs, another button, and get delivery of food, get your Uber ride, every technical innovation has made us lazier. A good 30 to 35 minutes of exercise, four or five days a week is a must! There are various fitness websites and mobile applications available that recommend different workouts for your body type and goal setting. Most of them are free! However, please follow doctors' advice before taking up a physical regime. There aren't any set universal guidelines for the number of days for the workout duration.

Whether you are looking at weight loss, maintaining your fitness level, or looking at building muscle and mass, all depend on the outcome you want. It also depends upon your age, what is your current fitness level etc. So I leave it up to you. But let me tell you what works for me is five days a week regime, which varies between 45 minutes to an hour. I put in a lot of variation in my workout schedule and tend to keep it interesting as I get bored with the mundane. Every day is a different routine. Some days, I will do yoga, which I most definitely recommend. It has helped me tremendously, especially in stretching muscles I never knew existed! You need to build up your form and pose gradually. Care must be taken not to overstretch and tear muscles or cause injury to yourself. Many yoga practitioners are good at their jobs, and now thanks to the COVID19-pandemic, they are also teaching online. More and more research is being conducted on yoga and its health benefits. Some researches suggests that yoga can help regulate anxiety, depression, help with PTSD, allow for better sleep, help women suffering from cancer undergoing radiation therapy. Lower the cortisol levels, increase body awareness, decrease negative body image, and lower blood pressure.

Yoga can be used to help regulate anxiety and depression, improve mood and functioning, and help with those who have PTSD. Other studies suggest that yoga can assist with chronic insomnia. A 2006 study showed that yoga has an effect on body image for women. The women in the study objectified their bodies less after participation in the [yoga] program. Furthermore, among both men and women, more frequent yoga practice was associated with increased body awareness, positive affect, and satisfaction with life and decreased negative affect. Other studies like "Effectiveness of Yoga for Hypertension: Systematic Review and Meta-Analysis" has shown that "Yoga can be preliminarily recommended as an effective intervention for reducing blood pressure." [4]

We have the lymphatic fluid system in our body. It is part of the immune system. It helps in protecting the body from illness invaders, aids in digestion, and removing cellular waste. It does not have a pump like the heart for pushing the lymphatic fluid. For the circulation of lymphatic fluid, you need to move and exercise. It is that simple! Some latest studies suggests that long hours of sitting on your backside equates to smoking, So get yourself moving. Be innovative. You can use your body weight for exercises like squat, pull-ups, push-ups, and lunges. You can even do spot jogging. You can watch thousands of aerobic videos for beginners on the internet. There are no excuses! Make your fitness program. I suggest you giving your body once in a while a few surprises, doing something different in the workout, changing your routine suddenly,

[4] https://www.quora.com/search?q=benefits%20of%20yoga

stepping up the pace of the routine, basically having fun with your workout out sessions, don't make it a struggle. Even taking your pets for a walk would do you wonders.

The next most crucial thing for Physical health is the fuel that your body needs. Yes, I will talk about your nutrition. And again, there are a lot of nutritionists out there who might help you to get into shape. For me, nutrition is not a fad diet. It's a total lifestyle change. A very close nutritionist made this statement once, and I agree that eating right has to be a lifestyle change and a sincere commitment to stick to treat your body like a temple. I guarantee you if you take care of your body, the body will take care of you. It all depends on what you put in; excellent input equals excellent output. It can be compared to putting diesel oil into an unleaded patrol car and expect it to run- that ain't happening!

The primary nutrients that your body needs in a balanced amount are Protein, Carbs, Fats, Vitamins, and minerals. Having a balanced diet is extremely important. Get a lot of leafy vegetables, greens, and fruits in your diet every day. I take a handful of dried fruit nuts, almonds, Macadamia nuts, a few cashews, pistachios, peanuts unsalted, and roasted if I feel like snacking during the day. I also eat a mixture of seeds like sunflower, pumpkin, chia, and flax when I am hungry. It keeps you satiated for an extended period of time. One should do blending. Take a few green vegetables like baby spinach, celery, cucumber, broccoli, and herbs like dill leaves, coriander, parsley, and blend it, not juice it. Blending retains the fibre; that's why I prefer it to juicing. The idea is to keep your body at a healthy alkaline level, and when your body is in an alkaline state, the disease does not exist! Understandably, junk food in your diet needs to be avoided. You need to avoid packaged foods. You need to avoid those carbonated sugary drinks. If you have a sweet tooth, there are so many sugar substitutes available that you can use, like organic jaggery, palm sugar, and raw organic honey. Please consult your doctor; if you have diabetes, please take advice before getting into a nutritional plan. It is never too late to change your diet and the way you eat. It's said that if you follow a routine for 21 days, it forms a habit. You will see remarkable changes within your body once you inculcate these habits.

The next aspect I would like to touch on is water intake, and not many of us drink enough water. There is no guideline on how much water you need to drink, but your body should get 2 to 3 litres daily on average. Blood is made out of essentially water. Water flushes out toxins from the body. Water also prevents early signs of wrinkles. It helps in cleansing the internal organs. Three-fourth of our body is made out of water; thus, you can imagine water's importance and its role in managing physical well-being. And not just that, water also helps in weight loss as, a minimum of 30 minutes before a meal one should have water, which prevents overeating during your meal. Most of the time, when we are hungry, we don't know whether we are hungry or thirsty.

Water is vital, and I can't stress this enough! Patients who are on dialysis and have kidney-related issues, please take advice from your doctor. Remember juices, teas cannot be the substitute for plain drinking water. Get your glass of water now!

Nowadays, the vegetables and herbs that grow in soils are nutrient deprived. So you need to supplement your body with essential minerals and supplements. Get your dose of multi Vitamins. Get in your Vitamin A, C, and E. Lot of us are Vitamin D deficient, so we need the supplement for that. I take B12 supplements that I don't get from animal protein as I am vegetarian. Please do your blood test to check for any vitamin deficiency and consult your nutritionist, doctor to get on a vitamin and supplement program.

There has always been a great debate between eating vegetarian and non-vegetarian food. I'm not going to add much over there, but I've been a vegetarian for quite some time, and I can see a lot of difference in terms of energy levels in me. And when I go to sleep at night, I go empty or relatively on a very light stomach, which makes me feel good and gives my digestive system a break, and all the energy is utilized for healing and restoration of the body during sleep. I mean, I am not against those who eat and love their meat. By all means, eat, but I'm just implying that you keep a portion of vegetables on a higher side in your diet. This is my key takeaway.

"Vegetarians appear to have lower low-density lipoprotein cholesterol levels, lower blood pressure, and lower hypertension and type 2 diabetes rates than meat-eaters. Eggetarians also tend to have a lower body mass index, lower overall cancer rates, and lower chronic disease risk."[5]

One can also follow the circadian diet, which makes so much sense. The circadian rhythm diet is also known as the body clock diet. "It is[6] a form of time-

---

[5] https://wwws.fitnessrepublic.com/nutrition/
    healthy-eating/pros-and-cons-of-vegetarianism.html

[6] https://www.forbes.com/sites/nomanazish/2020/02/29/
    everything-you-need-to-know-about-the-circadian-rhythm-
    diet/

restricted eating plan where you eat in sync with this internal clock. This means that you eat during the daylight hours, within a window of 12 hours or less, and fast for the remaining 12 or more hours each day." You start with heavy meals for breakfast and end on lighter dinner meals.

Let's now discuss body talk. Your body goes through all the rigmarole of life every day until you die. The least you can do is be grateful to it for it. There is a beautiful gratitude exercise. You start from your head, going right up to your toes and being thankful. For example, you can touch your skull and say I thank the skull, which handles all the essential Motor and neurological functions in my body. Then you come to your eyes and say thank you for making me able to see the beauty in the world, the beauty in everything to enjoy the beautiful nature in all its grandeur, and the good in people. Then thank the nose for being able to smell the beautiful aroma of the food being cooked or the lovely smell of a flower or the smell of the first raindrop falling on mother earth during the monsoon, anything just innovative. You can improvise as you grow along. Then you can thank your mouth for being able to express feelings and express thoughts through words. You can go on doing this right down to your toes, and you will see an amazing kind of sense of well-being as beautiful sensations being felt in your body. One should make it a daily habit, possibly at night. Another useful technique is just before going to sleep, say three things you did for your body that helped. You could say, for example, I walked today, I put in nutritional food, had a fair amount of water. Just mention three good things that you did for your body. This is the last thought your body hears before going to sleep. Trust me; your body will thank you for it!

These are some of the things listed above that one should practice for physical well-being and health. The body's got its intelligence. There are trillions and trillions of cells in our body, liver cells, heart cells, pancreatic cells, kidney cells, and their intelligence on taking care. Enjoy your body. It is designed for health. Stay positive, stay healthy, feed-in positive emotions and thought, and feeding your body with the right nutrients. What your body can do will surely amaze you. I witnessed dramatic changes. I am more energetic in my life than I have ever been. I go for trekking, hiking, easily run a 12k to 14 K distance. I swam the Swimathon, which is 5k in a -25metre pool, I even went on to swim 7k in the sea. I feel like a young, energetic kid once again. Stay energetic!

Chapter 8
MENTAL AND EMOTIONAL HEALTH

THERE IS A STRONG MIND-BODY connection. What thoughts you entertain in mind reflects directly on your body. Mental and emotional well-being is an exhaustive topic. Still, in this chapter, I will try and cut it short and discuss a few fundamental techniques that you could use and inculcate in your daily routine. Thoughts are the language of your mind, and emotions are the language of your body. Your first experience comes in the form of a thought that comes in your awareness, and then you identify with it. The more you believe in it, the more energy you give to it, which translates into your body as emotions, which you experience, and again those emotions get reflected into your thoughts. These thoughts feed your emotions again, the cycle repeats, and most probably, this cycle is a vicious one!

To reiterate the above, let's do an exercise right now. Shut your eyes and think about a thought; let's go with a positive thought. Think of a positive thought that you can bring back from memory, perhaps from far away and perhaps from long ago. While entertaining this thought, consciously experience what you went through in this thought, the people involved, dialogues transpired, and feel the thought with your five senses. Make the experience as real as possible. You will soon observe emotions related to this thought that will come into your experience.

The feel-good sensations that you sense are a positive one and your body chemistry changes. It feels nice! Now the opposite transpires If you do the exercise with a negative thought. You create those same experiences and feel the uneasy ones with your senses. These translate to negative emotional experiences, and your body chemistry changes again. This is how the process works from my perspective. So it is of utmost importance to take care of your thoughts. We need to take care of it, as they are our emotional experiences' root cause. You take care at the root level, and the emotions accordingly get aligned. On average, human beings have 70 to 75 thousand thoughts, and most of them are negative. Now more work is required for treating negative thought patterns. We should take care of these self-inflicting patterns.

Negative thoughts examples can be- why did it go wrong? Why me? Am I deserving? Why is it so hard for me? We often put ourselves in negative scenarios and negative patterns and paths, and it's okay because we all are human at the end of the day. Don't criticize yourself too much and stress yourself. There is definitely a way out of this all!

When you have a good mental health, you have a sense of satisfaction. You have an enthusiastic approach to life, you live life to the fullest, you laugh, you get the ability to fight off adversity and bounce back, you find a balance between work and play, you have self-confidence and high self-esteem, you want to learn new skills, and you have an excellent capability to adapt the ability to build and maintain fulfilling relationships.

Let's work on how do we get rid of these negative thought cycles? Here are four techniques that I would like to discuss with you on this. The first technique is what I call "being equanimous". So what happens in this is that you need to step back and just be aware when you experience a thought. Don't identify with this thought; do not give it any energy, do not associate with it. Just observe it neutrally. Give it space, let the thought move around in that space, and then just let it go. This method is called being equanimous; it's also called in therapies, cognitive diffusion. It is a great technique and works wonders. One can also label the thought when you step behind and observe. So, for example, if you have a thought as such, say I'm writing this book, and I get a thought" "what is he talking about as if he's mastered it all" catch the thought and label it as "Mister know it all thought". You can step back from the thought and you can be equanimous and also at the same time label it. Once you give it a label, you have a disassociation with the thought. Keep working on these thought patterns; don't give your attention to these anymore, and they will soon cease to have power over you. It might come again and again, and the less and less energy or attention you give to the thought, you have less and less identification. The thought comes, but now it loses its juice. This is how one can help get rid of these negative repetitive thought patterns. If you can properly divert your mind to think something fruitful, negative thoughts are bound to vanish. Another analogy would be, think of birds in the sky. The birds are the thoughts, and your awareness and space is the vastness of the sky in which the thoughts, i.e., the birds are flying. Try it yourself. Don't just take my word for it.

The second technique is to "be present." What I mean by being present is that when you get stuck into a negative thought cycle and are unable to disassociate away from the thought pattern by observing from a neutral point of view because the thought is sticky, then you try being present in the moment. Being present means getting out of the mental dialogue and being present in the situation you are currently in, using all your senses, such as feeling the chair if you're sitting, observing the sounds you hear, and any smell that you become aware of. Just be in the NOW, be present. If there is any conversation happening around, you can pay attention to that as well. Be fully present in that situation with all your senses. Once you do that, all your energies are involved in being in the present moment, and then there is no energy or space left for mental dialogue. So try and BE PRESENT and live in the NOW. Make this a habit!

The third technique is mindfulness meditation, i.e. follow your breath-meditation technique. Here you observe your breath. Sit in a folded leg position, keep the spine straight, and focus on observing the breath. Which nostril is the air hitting first while breathing?. Can you follow the breath right down till the diaphragm and then observe it while coming out? How is the breath? Is it a shallow breath?. Is it a long breath? Does it feel cool? Is it warm? Is there rapid breathing? Slow breathing? You are just observing the breath and nothing else. If any thought comes, you ignore and focus back on the breath. This breath technique meditation is taught in Vipassana. It's called the Anapana Meditation. Mindfulness meditation with breath is a beautiful tool. When you practice this, you cultivate more awareness, and you indulge less in the mental dialogue. This is a path-breaking technique for some.

The fourth technique is "questioning the thought." It is logical reasoning with your thoughts. So when there is a thought pattern in which you are being haunted, the only thing you need to do is to question the thought. The first question you need to ask is, is this thought useful to me? Follow it up with, is this thought the ultimate truth? How do you know absolutely that this thought is the truth? Is this the truth, or is my mind just making up stories from an old habit and blabbering. Your questioning the thought is putting your conscious mind in control. You put yourself in control rather than following a negative subconscious pattern, and then you can quickly change the questioning from negative to positive and say, what can I learn from this thought? Is there any effective action that I can take from this thought pattern? What is the thought pattern teaching me? You start shifting your focus from negative to positive things in your life, and then you reach an optimistic frame of mind. That's how you can turn your energies from a negative state of being to a positive state of being. It's not easy. It's not a quick fix. You need to work on yourself, and you need to practice changing this behaviour pattern. The negative thought patterns can be compared to the grooves on a record player. The more similar patterns we entertain, the deeper the grooves on the record player. This is also termed neuroplasticity. The idea is to change those negative thought patterns into positive behaviours and attitudes, to change the grooves on the record player, and thus play a better song of life. Therefore change your belief and hence your reality. Once you take care of these thought patterns, it automatically flows well into your emotional well-being, translating into positive emotional well-being.

Now for your emotional well-being, a lot can be done. But taking care of the thought is of prime importance, and the subsequent by-product will be an emotion that would be happy and joyous. To lift your emotional well-being, you can listen to good music. You can do creative work that you always wanted to do but delayed it, either by painting or pick up a skill or learn something new, or be in nature, which is a fantastic therapy by itself. A lot of people do a lot of journaling. You can keep a gratitude journal; all this helps you get into the right emotional state. Good emotional well-being will feed into our thought patterns. Then the positive thought will feed into your emotions, and hopefully, you now get into a cycle of better emotional well-being. It takes a lot of effort. It's not easy. You need to take onus, and you need to work for it. Once you start the process, the fruits of the process become sweet and delicious.

Chapter 9
ENERGY HEALTH

WE HAVE ALREADY SPOKEN AND discussed physical, mental, and emotional well-being, but what about our soul? Taking care of our spiritual energy is of vital importance. The spiritual is the energy source of all physical manifestations.

Let us talk about energy! What is Energy? Everything around us, everything that we see, touch, and feel, even ourselves, i.e., our physical bodies, even our thoughts. Everything is made up of energy, and science has proved it beyond doubt that everything is made out of this. Anything that you see and perceive can be broken up into its molecular structure. We can go further break the molecule down into its atomic structure. When we break the atom further down, you have its nucleus with electrons revolving around it. There is an analogy that if you take a nucleus of an atom to the pinhead's size, then the first electron revolving around the nucleus is 60 feet apart! That just shows that %99.999999999999, that is 12 decimal places is just space, and the remaining portion, which is %0.000000000001 is matter.

So everything mostly contains space! It is just a mind-blowing revelation, isn't it? Do you think that God lacked creativity, that there is the vastness of space that exists which is of no use? No! quantum physics is proved that this space consists of potential energy present everywhere, which connects everything and permeates all matter. We can call this energy as "Chi" in the Chinese, "Mana" in the Hawaiian culture, "Prana" in the yogic culture. This energy can be utilized and harnessed for our well-being. We need to understand the dance of the unseen energy!

We should take up spiritual practices in our daily lives to harnesses this Energy. This energy is freely available to us to use for one's spiritual growth and well-being. There are a lot of courses accessible.

I recommend the following; Qigong exercise. It is a form of gentle exercise. "Qigong is composed of movements that are typically repeated, strengthening and stretching the body, increasing fluid movement (blood, synovial, and lymph), enhancing balance and proprioception, and improving the awareness of how the body moves through space".[7]

Tai chi is another form of exercise that began as a Chinese tradition. It's based on martial arts and involves slow movements and deep breaths. Tai chi

[7] Wikipedia qigong

has many physical and emotional benefits. "Some of the benefits of "tai chi" include decreased anxiety and depression and improvements in cognition."[8]

Then you could take up "reiki". "Reiki is a form of alternative medicine called energy healing. Reiki practitioners use a technique called palm healing or hands-on healing through which 'universal energy' is said to be transferred through the palms of the practitioner to the patient to encourage emotional or physical healing."[9]

"There is Magnified healing. Magnified Healing® establishes a constant flow of energy from your heart to the Source, the All That Is, the Infinite Mind, the GOD MOST HIGH OF THE UNIVERSE, through all of the Spiritual Centers, down to the Diamond at the Center of the Earth. The link spirals and brings a deep state of grace pulsing forth from you the source, laying the very foundation for the

---

[8] https://www.healthline.com/health/tai-chi-benefits
[9] https://www.physioinmotionnb.com/reiki

Ascension process."[10]

You can take up tapping, which is tapping into the energy meridians flow just below the surface of your body to release unblocked energies. Some studies had shown EFT tapping to be useful for anxiety, pain, and cravings when the practice was self-applied: Health care workers who practiced EFT tapping were found to have decreased ratings of pain, emotional distress, and cravings just two hours after tapping.

You can learn about the chakra balancing technique and energizing them to restore balance and healing on all levels. It's necessary to forge something for yourself at your energy level, the source of all. There are also healing modalities at the energy level, such as Bach Flower remedies that work on the emotional energy body. There is aromatherapy that uses essential oils from various parts of plants for healing.

[10]https://rogeransanelli.com/magnified-healing/

Go out there and get yourself familiarized with energy activation practices and use them in your life. Enrich your life!

Chapter 10
THE BREATH

THE BREATH IS YOUR FRIEND for life, from the moment you are born with the first inhalation to the moment you die with the last exhalation. We are not at all conscious about the breath. Observe, when you are stressed, anxious, under a panic attack notice, how your breath changes, and when you are calm and relaxed and feeling good, notice how your breath moves. Be aware of this best friend of yours. Deep equal breath is the way to go! We never breathe from the diaphragm but typically take shallow breaths from the chest area, which is not good. When we exhale, we do not exhale fully; there are still toxins that need to be released. I can't tell you how beneficial it is to have a breathing exercise routine in your daily life. It is merely not an inhalation and exhalation cycle; a lot of magic happens during breathing.

In this chapter, I'm going to be discussing breathing. It is freely available to us! The best things in life are indeed free. Breath is a tool that one can use to their advantage for obtaining optimal health. I will try and focus on a few breathing methodologies that you can inculcate in our daily routine if you're not doing it already. There is a whole lot of studies out there pointing out to advantages of breathing. It helps in improving the blood flow. It makes you feel energetic. It changes the body chemistry. It detoxifies your body. It stimulates the lymphatic system, and it also is known to cure PTSD -post-traumatic stress disorder symptoms.

Let's start with the first breathing technique, and it's crucial because of the COVID19- pandemic situation, which has affected all of us. Naturally, due to COVID19-, many people nowadays, at the onset of the slightest symptoms, whether it's a cough, fever, or a slight headache, automatically start thinking the worst, and your anxiety goes up. People start getting stressed and anxious, your breathing becomes erratic, and you might end up having palpitations even. These are the typical signs of anxiety and panic attacks. Before you pop that pill, I suggest trying these breathing techniques that I will share with you. It's effortless! The first technique is called BOX BREATHING. It is simple you inhale for four counts, hold for four counts, exhale for four counts, and then again hold for four counts. You can start with lower counts based on your comfort level. You could do this with three counts as well or two counts, whatever seems agreeable to you. But equal counts on inhalations, holding, exhalation, and holding thereafter. You can start with four rounds and go up to 6 rounds. Once done, rest assured that you will experience a calming effect and relax your nervous system.

The second technique is quite related to the first one since your anxiety and stress levels are high, a lot of mind chatter prevails, then sleeping at night becomes a challenge for many people. The majority of the population suffers from insomnia. Lack of sleep or rather lack of quality sleep is harmful to your body. Sleep is when the body rejuvenates and repairs. Now, this breathing technique is called the 8-4 breathing technique, which helps you fall asleep. In this technique, you breathe in for four counts, and then you exhale through your mouth, making a pursed-lip as if you're blowing out a candle for eight counts. Now, these counts again depend upon your comfort level. You can breathe in for three counts, breathe out with a pursed-lip for six-count, or you can breathe in for two counts, breathe out through pursed lips for four counts. You can slowly keep on increasing the counts, inhale for six, and exhale for 12 counts. Do five or six rounds of this exercise. This breathing to be done just before you sleep. It calms you down, slows your heartbeat, and you're probably will be going to sleep in the middle of the routine! You won't even realize it! This is a proven technique that I have been doing in, and it works amazingly. These are the typical breathing exercises related to anxiety and panic attacks that subsequently lead to sleeping disorders.

Now, let's cover three of the incredible yogic breathing exercise. It is imperative that this yogic breathing is done on an empty stomach. So you need to have the last meal or anything liquid a couple of hours before delving into this.

The first type of breathing is called fire breathing as well as Bhastrika pranayama.

- Sit in vajrasana or sukhasana (cross-legged position).

- (Pranayama can be more effective in vajrasana

as your spine is straight up and the diaphragmatic movement is better.)

- Make a fist and fold your arms, placing them near your shoulders.

- Inhale deeply, raise your hands straight up and open your fists.

- Exhale slightly forcefully, bring your arms down next to your shoulders and close your fists.

- Continue for 20 breaths.

- Relax with palms on your thighs.

- Take a few normal breaths.

- Continue for two more rounds.[11]

You can also visualize while exhaling. You can think about taking out all the anxiety, stress, negative feeling, and emotions in our body. You can start slow. Do three sets of ten at the start, and you can slowly increase it as per your comfort level. What are the advantages of this breath? It takes out the excess

---

11https://www.artofliving.org/in-en/yoga/breath-ing-technique/bhastrika-pranayam

phlegm in your lungs. It oxygenates your blood. It renews energy. It energizes your mind and body, and also it calms the mind and brings your inner sense to the present moment.

"The next yogic breathing is the Kapal Bhati.

1. Sit comfortably with your spine erected. Place your hands on the knees with palms open to the sky.

2. Take a deep breath.

3. As you exhale, pull your stomach. Pull your navel in back towards the spine. Do as much as you comfortably can. You may keep your right hand on the stomach to feel the abdominal muscles contract.

4. As you relax the navel and the abdomen, the breath flows into your lungs automatically.

5. Take 20 such breaths to complete one round of Kapal Bhati Pranayama.

6. After completing the round, relax with your eyes closed and observe the sensations in your body.

7. Do two more rounds of Kapal Bhati Pranayama."

"4 Tips for Kapal Bhati Beginners:

- The exhalation in the Skull Shining Breathing technique is active and forceful. So, just throw out your breath.

- Don't worry about the inhalation. The moment you relax your abdominal muscles, inhalation will happen naturally.

- Keep your awareness on breathing out.

- Practice this technique at home on an empty stomach."

"8 Benefits of Kapal Bhati Pranayama:

1. Increases the metabolic rate and aids in weight loss

2. Clears the nadis (subtle energy channels)

3. Stimulates abdominal organs and thus is extremely useful to those with diabetes

4. Improves blood circulation and adds radiance to the face

5. Improves digestive tract functioning, absorption, and assimilation of nutrients

6. Results in a taut and trimmed down belly

7. Energizes the nervous system and rejuvenates brain cells

8. Calms and uplifts the mind"

"Who should avoid doing Kapal Bhati Pranayama:

Avoid practicing this breathing technique if you have an artificial pacemaker or stent, epilepsy, hernia, backache due to slip disc, or have recently undergone abdominal surgery."[12]

"The next yogic breath is the ANULOM VILOM METHOD

The third type of breathing is shamanic breathing, quantum breathing, or energy breathing. Under this classification comes WIM HOF breathing. While sitting in a comfortable place, take 30 quick, deep breaths, inhaling through your nose and exhaling through your mouth. Then, take a deep breath and exhale; hold until you need to breathe in. Inhale again, as deep as you can, and hold it for 10 seconds.

---

[12] https://www.artofliving.org/in-en/yoga/breath-ing-techniques/skull-shining-breath-kapal-bhati

Repeat as many times as you like[13]. I've been doing it for more than a year now, and it has helped me a lot. It alkalizes your body. It energizes your body. It releases the feel-good dopamine in your body. You can feel this oxygenation running throughout your body. It's just a fantastic routine. I advise seeing the online YouTube tutorial for WIM HOF and under supervision as it can get intense.

Breathing is an essential tool for rejuvenating the mind and the body and it should be a part of our well-being regime.

---

[13] https://www.discovermagazine.com/health/can-breath-ing-like-wim-hof-make-us-superhuman

THE END?

Chapter 11
THE QUEST

IN THE PRECEDING CHAPTERS, WE discussed various techniques to achieve well-being at physical, mental, emotional, and spiritual energy levels. I keep my trust that you will make it a promise to include the routines in your daily life, which have been discussed with you.

When one decides to take responsibility for their being, tremendous energy surges through them -a feeling of empowerment, ecstasy, and liveliness can be experienced. All that I have mentioned in this book is nothing but a cleansing process which helps in detoxifying your body and releasing unwanted energies and emotions from your being. Once you are clean on all levels of existence, you start being susceptible to higher energies, frequencies, and wisdom accessible from the Universal Mind.

Let me explain. We can only see specific colours in the rainbow, we can only hear certain sounds, and all are within a range that is perceived by our sensory perceptions. It's like going into a dark room or a warehouse with a torchlight. You can only see objects on which light is thrown, and this is similar to your perception. But what if the entire warehouse or the room lights are switched on together, bang! You get exposed to a lot more than you can ever imagine! You gain a broader perspective of everything.

When one goes through the internal and external metamorphosis at the physical and spiritual levels,

SOUL2SOUL SESSIONS WITH AB EPISODE1

Do nutritional supplements play a vital role in boosting immunity, and could it help fight the current pandemic? This and much more will be discussed with our nutritional minerals and supplements specialist Mike Tolani. Please scan the QR code.

SOUL2SOUL SESSIONS WITH AB EPISODE 2

Which is the best diet for me? Is intermittent fasting good? Should we be avoiding carbs completely? This and much more will be discussed with our expert Ms. Kamna Bhandari. Please scan the QR code.

SOUL2SOUL SESSIONS WITH AB EPISODE 3

"Everyone's been talking about keeping physical health optimal and boosting immunity to fight COVID19- pandemic. What about the mental fight against this virus?" How can we be mentally strong during these challenging times? Let's discuss COVID19- RESILIENCE with our expert Shraddha Sidhwani. Please scan the QR code.

SOUL2SOUL SESSIONS WITH AB EPISODE 4

The most powerful sources of information come from within, and TAROT aids in coming in contact with one's higher self and the cosmic for guidance. Let's discuss TAROT methodology with our expert, Leenata Shah. Please scan the QR code.

SOUL2SOUL SESSIONS WITH AB EPISODE 5

"The power of Nadi and the diagnosis through Nadi Pariksha (pulse diagnosis)." Nadi Pariksha, a tool to guide you through your life entirely on a different plane of consciousness. Join this power-packed session with our expert Ravi Krishnamurthy. Please scan the QR code.

SOUL2SOUL SESSIONS WITH AB EPISODE 6

Our physical body and why they produce pain! Join this insightful session with our expert Dr. Raashi Khatri Panjabi, MD – Orofacial pain, Headaches, and TMJ disorders. Please scan the QR code.

SOUL2SOUL SESSIONS WITH AB EPISODE 7

You are the PLACEBO! Let's talk about self-healing modalities and empower yourself. Join in on an awe-inspiring session with our expert Ronak Gujjar, wellness and meditation coach and a business strategist. Please scan the QR code.

SOUL2SOUL SESSIONS WITH AB EPISODE 8

Bach flower remedies and how they help to heal our emotional issues! Let's discover this genie in a bottle with our amazing therapist Gita Hariani. Please scan the QR code.

SOUL2SOUL SESSIONS WITH AB EPISODE 9

Want to release limiting thoughts and beliefs? have a clear thought process? Find the right family dynamics? Want healing at all levels!? Let's discover regression and family constellation therapy with Rashmi Gupta Gheewala. Please scan the QR code.

SOUL2SOUL SESSIONS WITH AB EPISODE 10

Energy healing addresses the illness caused due to disturbances in the energy flow in the body. When energy flow is fixed, the person is on the way to recovery. Let's understand this wonderful healing modality with Gayatri Panjabi. Please scan the QR code.

SOUL2SOUL SESSIONS WITH AB EPISODE 11

Live your ideal life despite the current trying times. Manifest your reality now! How? Let's find out with inspirational speaker & entrepreneur Shreans Daga. Please scan the QR code.

Acknowledgements

First and foremost, I would like to thank the universal power, the source of all manifestations, God, whatever name you would like to call, my inspiration in putting this book together. I always wanted to write a book on my learnings, and the COVID19- pandemic has acted as a catalyst and enabled me to put my internal thoughts into action. I realized writing this book was so therapeutic. I visited some dark phases of my life, which I needed for my personal and spiritual growth.

I would like to thank my wife, Neetu, from the bottom of my heart for planting the idea of the book in my mind. You have given me the power to believe in my passion, pursue my dreams, and helped me with some creative and practical suggestions during this phase.

To all the teachers who came into my life, the relationships I encountered. All the relationships in my life have been a great teacher. I would like to thank my friends I have made along this journey of mine called life, the distinguished authors of all books that I have read, and the video logs of the spiritual gurus.

To 24by7 Publishing, for trusting me and putting this book out there for the world to read.

December, 2020   Amit Butani

Author Bio

Amit Butani is an accomplished marketing professional working in a travel retail organization. He has a Bachelor's degree in Electronics and Engineering and a Post-Graduate MBA degree in Finance from the UK. His true passion lies in the study of spiritual sciences. He is married to his soul mate; he met her while she was only 14, and he was 16 years old. They have two beautiful kids, a daughter, and a son, respectively, aged 10 and 11. He currently lives in Mumbai, India. His love for the mystical has led him to take on various healing modalities. He is a certified life coach, Eden energy medicine practitioner, and EFT/TFT certified practitioner, a certified aromatherapist with a diploma in Akashic records. His spiritual thirst continues, and he calls himself a 'work in progress'. He has undertaken various breathing courses like the Science of Life & Breath from the Pratibimb Charitable Trust, undergone Dopamine Activated Breathing (DAB) course by Marcel Hof, Transcendental Meditation Breath Work by the Pyramid Valley Institute based in India, and active breath practitioner of Wim Hof Breathing Technique. He is a fitness enthusiast, plays the tabla and the guitar. Loves to be in nature, loves going for treks and hikes. This book attempts to reach out to all who are willing to empower themselves and take responsibility for their well-being on all levels of existence, i.e., physical, mental, emotional & spiritual level, to enjoy life to its fullest.

Love this book? Don't forget to leave a review!

Every review matters, and it matters a *lot!*

Head over to Amazon or wherever you purchased this book to leave an honest review for me.

I thank you endlessly.

You can send in your reviews also to amitbutani@gmail.com

BOOKS FOR FURTHER READING & RESEARCH

1. Tomorrow's God – Neale Donald Walsch

2. Happiness begins at home – Daisaku Ikeda with Kaneko Ikeda

3. Krishna, The man and his philosophy – OSHO

4. Higher Self Now – William Buhlman

5. Living with the Himalayan Masters – Swami Rama

6. Light from many lamps – Eichler Watson

7. You are the Placebo – Dr. Joe Dispenza

8. The journey home – Autobiography of an American Swamy – Radhanath Swami

9. What if this is heaven – Anita Morrjani

10. Ramtha – The White Book

11. The Celestine prophecy – James Redfield

12. Your sacred self – Wayne W. Dyer

13. IAM THAT – Sri Nisargadatta Maharaj

14. Inner Engineering – A yogi's guide to joy – Sadhguru

15. Becoming supernatural – Dr. Joe Dispenza

16. Conversations with God series – Neale Donald Walsch

17. Vibrational healing through the Chakras – Joy Gardner

18. The cosmic power within you – Joesph Murphy

19. Mysteries of Mind over Matter – compilation by Ved Prakash

20. Laws of the spirit world – Khorshed Bhavnagari

21. The Biology of Belief – Bruce H. Lipton